FROM SUFFRAGISTS TO SENATORS:

A Century of Laws by Women Since 1920

Dorothy Patton

For my foremothers, Sophy, Vina, Winnie, Disey, Ella, Mamie Celestra, Marguerite, Patience, Dolly, Etta, Axuel and Pat, whose faith and fortitude I channel every day.

Acknowledgments

I gratefully acknowledge the outstanding primary sources that are available through the National Archives, the Library of Congress, the U.S. House of Representatives, and the U.S. Government Publishing Office. The collections and the federal employees who manage them are national treasures. I hope that readers are inspired to tap into these rich resources. I am grateful to a wonderful circle of friends and family who supported this project, especially my loving husband, Jason.

The right of citizens of the United States to vote shall not be denied or abridged by the United States or by any State on account of sex.

Congress shall have power to enforce this article by appropriate legislation.

19TH AMENDMENT TO THE U.S. CONSTITUTION
(August 18, 1920)

Foreword

Years before 55 men gathered in Philadelphia to write the U.S. Constitution, Abigail Adams wrote a letter to her husband John. She advised the men laying the foundation of American government to:

Remember the Ladies, and be more generous and favourable to them than your ancestors. Do not put such unlimited power into the hands of the Husbands. Remember all Men would be tyrants if they could.[i]

Amused, John quickly wrote back, "As to your extraordinary Code of Laws, I cannot but laugh."[ii] But weeks later, he took Abigail seriously and wrote to a friend:

Depend upon it, sir, it is dangerous ... to alter the Qualifications of Voters. There will be no End of it. New Claims will arise. Women will demand a Vote. Lads from 12 to 21 will think their Rights not enough attended to, and every Man, who has not a Farthing, will demand an equal Voice ... .[iii]

Abigail and John were both right. Forgotten voters would rise up, but it would take 133 years and a constitutional amendment to ensure that America remembered "the Ladies."

Part I of this booklet remembers the struggle for women's suffrage. One hundred years ago, the courage and persistence of visionary women and men culminated in the 19th Amendment to the U.S. Constitution. Part II surveys some of the legislative accomplishments of women in each decade since suffrage. Women leaders ended child labor, expanded access to higher education, funded medical research, and much more. Part III looks to the next hundred years and implores women and men to exercise their precious right to vote. Only then can our democracy truly represent "We the People."

PART I
THE ROAD TO SUFFRAGE

"'We the People?' Which 'We the People?' The women were not included."

-Lucy Stone
(1853)

Source: Linda T. Monk, *The Words We Live By, Your Annotated Guide to the Constitution* (Hyperion 2003), 12

The men who drafted the U.S. Constitution in the summer of 1787 spoke passionately about "government by the people." Yet they did not define "the people" who would participate in the new American democracy. The original Constitution addressed who could vote in only one circumstance – the election of the federal House of Representatives - and it left the decision to the states.[iv] In most states, that meant that only white, land-owning men could vote. Thus, the first form of America's democracy included only a small minority of America's people.

Early Suffrage by States

All New Jersey residents worth fifty pounds, including women, were allowed to vote under the state's 1776 constitution. But in 1807, the state legislature limited voting rights to tax-paying, white male citizens.

Wyoming Territory gave women the right to vote in 1869 to encourage western settlement.

Women in the Utah Territory had the right to vote in 1870, then lost it in 1887, then won it back when Utah became a state in 1896.

Sources: https://www.nps.gov/articles/voting-rights-in-nj-before-the-15th-and-19th.htm; https://www.nps.gov/articles/wyoming-women-s-history.htm; https://www.nps.gov/articles/utah-women-s-history.htm (April 20, 2019)

Seneca Falls, 1848

More than 300 suffragists, including Elizabeth Cady Stanton, Lucretia Mott and Frederick Douglass, convened the First Women's Rights Convention in Seneca Falls, New York. They knew that they may face "no small amount of ... ridicule," but they were resolved that women "have immediate admission to all the rights and privileges which belong to them as citizens of these United States." Their Declaration of Sentiments listed grievances including the inequality of women in education, pay, employment, criminal justice, marriage, divorce, and property ownership. Brilliantly, they echoed an earlier document:

We hold these truths to be self-evident; that all men and women are created equal; that they are endowed by their Creator with certain inalienable rights; that among these are life, liberty, and the pursuit of happiness; that to secure these rights governments are instituted, deriving their just powers from the consent of the governed.

Source: https://www.nps.gov/wori/learn/historyculture/declaration-of-sentiments.htm (April 16, 2019)

Eventually, the Constitution did describe the federal electorate, making it clear that women were not part of it. Ratified after the Civil War in 1868, the 14th Amendment penalized any state that denied "any of the male inhabitants of such State, being twenty-one years old, and citizens of the United States" the right to vote.[v]

The explicit exclusion of women energized Elizabeth Cady Stanton, Isabella Beecher Hooker, Susan B. Anthony and others. They formed the National Woman Suffrage Association, and in 1871, they petitioned the U.S. Congress, writing, "women who are allowed no vote and therefore no representation cannot truly be heard."[vi]

The suffragists became a nationwide force. They marched and published newspaper articles. They petitioned state and federal officials and went on hunger strikes. When they picketed in front of the White House, bystanders spat on them. Authorities arrested and imprisoned them. In 1873, a New York jury of 12 men found Susan B. Anthony guilty of "knowingly voting without having the lawful right to vote," and she was fined $100.[vii]

Through the hardships, they persisted.

The Suffrage Parade, 1913

Alice Paul, a 28-year-old Quaker from New Jersey, organized the National American Woman Suffrage Association (NAWSA) Procession in Washington, DC. It made national headlines, assembling thousands of suffragists, nine bands, 24 floats, and representatives from foreign countries and every U.S. state. The parade began with state delegations of white women, followed by white men, followed by "the Negro women section." Refusing to be relegated to the back, Ida B. Wells, a Chicago business owner and founder of the Alpha Suffrage Club, made her way to the Illinois delegates' section once the parade began.

The suffragists were tripped and grabbed by counter-protesters. Washington police officers taunted them, and hecklers asked the men in the parade, "Where are your skirts?" A crowd attending Woodrow Wilson's inauguration impeded the parade. Secretary of War Henry Stimson called a troop of cavalry from nearby Fort Myer to control the crowd. By the end of the afternoon, 100 marchers were hospitalized.

Source: Sheridan Harvey, "Marching for the Vote: Remembering the Woman Suffrage Parade of 1913," https://memory.loc.gov/ammem/awhhtml/aw01e/aw01e.html, (April 16, 2019)

Official Program – Woman Suffrage Procession, cover illustration by Benjamin Dale for the National American Woman Suffrage Association parade, Washington, D.C.
Source: https://www.loc.gov/pictures/resource/ppmsca.12512/ (June 2, 2019)

Sixteen suffragists hike to Washington, D.C., for the 1913 Woman Suffrage Procession
Source: http: http://loc.gov/pictures/resource/cph.3a27602/ (June 2, 2019)

Nannie Burroughs and other African-American
women activists (1905-1915)
Source: https://www.loc.gov/item/93505051/ (May 10, 2019)

"Suffragettes" at the White House (1915-1920)
Source: http://www.loc.gov/pictures/item/2014703777/ (May
10, 2019)

Their unrelenting efforts paid off. In May of 1919, the House and the Senate approved a joint resolution to grant women the right to vote by constitutional amendment, but it had to be ratified by three-fourths of the states' legislatures. At the time, that meant 36 states had to ratify.

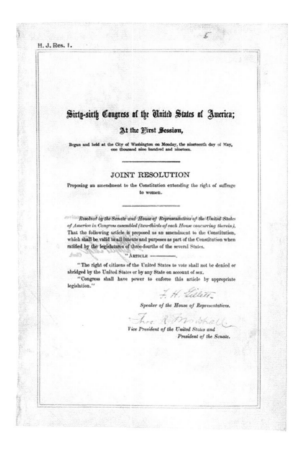

Source: https://www.archives.gov/files/historical-docs/doc-content/images/19th-amendment.pdf (May 10, 2019)

By the spring of 1920, 35 states had voted for the Amendment, and ratification seemed to come down to Tennessee, where the House of Representatives was deadlocked. Phoebe Ensminger Burn wrote a letter to her son, Tennessee State Representative Harry Burn, petitioning him to "be a good boy" and vote for women's suffrage.[viii] To the surprise of his Tennessee colleagues and the nation, Burn changed his vote, explaining, "I know that a mother's advice is always safest for her boy to follow, and my mother wanted me to vote for ratification."[ix]

Thus, on August 18, 1920, the 19th Amendment became the law of the land.

#	State	Date of Ratification	#	State	Date of Ratification
1	Illinois	June 10, 1919	19	Maine	Nov 5, 1919
2	Michigan	June 10, 1919	20	North Dakota	Dec 1, 1919
3	Wisconsin	June 10, 1919	21	South Dakota	Dec 4, 1919
4	Kansas	June 16, 1919	22	Colorado	Dec 15, 1919
5	New York	June 16, 1919	23	Kentucky	Jan 6, 1920
6	Ohio	June 16, 1919	24	Rhode Island	Jan 6, 1920
7	Pennsylvania	June 24, 1919	25	Oregon	Jan 13, 1920
8	Massachusetts	June 25, 1919	26	Indiana	Jan 16, 1920
9	Texas	June 28, 1919	27	Wyoming	Jan 27, 1920
10	Iowa	July 2, 1919	28	Nevada	Feb 7, 1920
11	Missouri	July 3, 1919	29	New Jersey	Feb 9, 1920
12	Arkansas	July 28, 1919	30	Idaho	Feb 11, 1920
13	Montana	Aug 2, 1919	31	Arizona	Feb 12, 1920
14	Nebraska	Aug 2, 1919	32	New Mexico	Feb 21, 1920
15	Minnesota	Feb 8, 1919	33	Oklahoma	Feb 28, 1920
16	New Hampshire	Sept 10, 1919	34	West Virginia	Mar 10, 1920
17	Utah	Oct 2, 1919	35	Washington	Mar 22, 1920
18	California	Nov 1, 1919	36	Tennessee	Aug 18, 1920

Sources: "Amendments to the Constitution of the United States of America," https://www. govinfo. gov/content/pkg/GPO-CONAN-1992/pdf/GPO-CONAN-1992-7.pdf, 36; "Washington State and the 19th Amendment," https://www.nps.gov/articles/washington-state-women-s-history.htm (April 16, 2019)

PART II
GAINING MOMENTUM DECADE BY DECADE

"I am no lady. I'm a Member of Congress, and I'll proceed on that basis."

-Rep. Mary Norton
(1925)

Source: https://history.house.gov/People/Detail/19024
(April 16, 2019)

Women in national leadership positions in the 1920s were small in numbers and lacked a cohesive agenda. Nevertheless, capitalizing on the momentum and organization of suffragist groups, they achieved some legislative victories.

Maternal and Pediatric Health

Originally sponsored by Montana Congresswoman Jeannette Rankin in 1918, the Sheppard-Towner Act of 1921 (Public Law 67-97) provided annual funding for healthcare for mothers and children. It focused on prenatal education and care of newborns in rural states. Although many women's groups supported the law, Oklahoma Representative Alice Mary Robertson opposed it as "dangerous class legislation, separating women from the men."[x]

Women's Citizenship

An American woman's citizenship was originally tied to her husband's. If she married a non-citizen, or if her husband renounced his American citizenship, she lost her citizenship. A group of 500,000 former suffragists, including the American Association of University Women, the Council of Jewish Women, the Daughters of the American Revolution, the Women's Christian Temperance Union, and the National League of Women Voters, lobbied for a change.[xi] Ohio Representative John Cable introduced the Married Women's Independent Citizenship Act (P.L. 67-346). "When the bill arrived at the Executive Mansion, President Harding found himself confronted by the demand of thousands of American women ... ."[xii] He signed it on September 22, 1922.

Women in Congress Tracker
1929 snapshot

70th Congress (1927-1929)

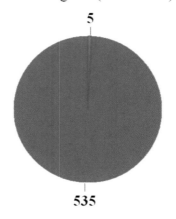

5

535

5 out of 540 total members

Following the stock market crash in 1929, the United States was plagued by soaring levels of unemployment, dangerous working conditions in factories, farms and mines, widespread child labor, and devastating levels of poverty. Women were strong supporters of a revolutionary package of laws that helped to get the nation back on its feet - the New Deal.

The women of the 71st Congress (1929–1931) pose on the Capitol steps. From left to right they are (front row) Pearl Oldfield of Arkansas, Edith Nourse Rogers of Massachusetts, Ruth Baker Pratt of New York, and Ruth Hanna McCormick of Illinois; (back row) Ruth Bryan Owen of Florida, Mary Norton of New Jersey, and Florence Kahn of California.

Source: https://history.house.gov/Exhibitions-and-Publications/WIC/Historical-Essays/No-Lady/Legislative-Interests/, image courtesy of the Library of Congress (April 19, 2019)

The Legacy of Eleanor Roosevelt

Eleanor Roosevelt began her public service by registering New York women to vote. As First Lady, she wrote a daily syndicated newspaper column, "My Day," held press conferences for women journalists, gave radio addresses, and campaigned for women candidates. Her influence on her husband's administration from 1933-1945 was clear. President Roosevelt appointed the first female cabinet member, Frances Perkins (Secretary of Labor), the first female U.S. ambassador, Ruth Bryan Owen (to Denmark), and the first female U.S. Court of Appeals judge (Sixth Circuit), Florence Allen. Eleanor Roosevelt's activism continues to inspire women to this day.

Source: https://history.house.gov/Exhibitions-andPublications/WIC/ Historical-Essays/National-Stage/Change-Continuity/; image courtesy of the Library of Congress (April 16, 2019)

Repeal of Prohibition

Almost immediately after the 18th Amendment prohibited "the manufacture, sale, or transportation of intoxicating liquors," it was clear that Prohibition's days were numbered. Although the Women's Christian Temperance Union had formed a massive lobby to address the crime, family dysfunction and poverty associated with excessive alcohol consumption, Prohibition was unpopular with many Americans.[xiii] It led to illegal bootlegging, international smuggling, and organized crime. In addition, the Great Depression made Congress desperate to stimulate the national economy. A group of women seeking relief for grain farmers supported the repeal of Prohibition. Rep. Mary Norton of New Jersey introduced the bill, and following state ratification, Prohibition was repealed by the 21st Amendment in 1933.[xiv]

Social Security

As the chair of President Roosevelt's Committee on Economic Security, Secretary of Labor Frances Perkins drafted the proposal that led to the Social Security Act of 1935 (P.L. 74-271).[xv] The program lifted Americans out of poverty during disability or old age, established maternal and child healthcare programs, and provided rehabilitation services to help people who were disabled on the job get back to work. Social Security continues to provide a critical safety net for millions of people.

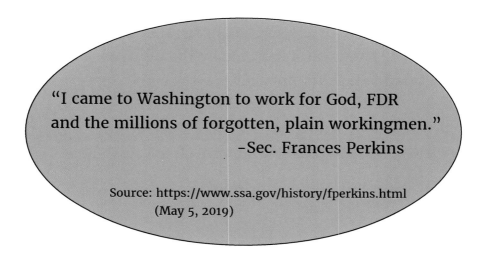

"I came to Washington to work for God, FDR and the millions of forgotten, plain workingmen."
–Sec. Frances Perkins

Source: https://www.ssa.gov/history/fperkins.html
(May 5, 2019)

Minimum Wage and Child Labor

House Labor Committee Chair Mary Norton and Secretary of Labor Frances Perkins worked with the Roosevelt Administration to create a fairer workplace. Courts and industry called their ideas unconstitutional, anti–competitive and violative of the right to contract. After years of debate, the Fair Labor Standards Act of 1938 (P.L. 75-718) mandated the first federal minimum wage of 25 cents per hour, a 40-hour work week, and an end to child labor.

Leading with Quiet Strength

In 1932 Hattie Wyatt Caraway of Arkansas was the first woman to be elected to the Senate. (Rebecca Latimer Felton was appointed by the Governor of Georgia to serve for one day in 1922.) Known as "Silent Hattie," she rarely spoke on the Senate floor, but she was a strong advocate for agricultural workers and for President Roosevelt's New Deal.

Sources: https://history.house.gov/People/Detail/13054; https://history.house.gov/People/Listing/C/Caraway,-Hattie-Wyatt-(C000138)/ (April 16, 2019)

Women in Congress Tracker
1939 snapshot

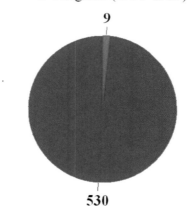

75th Congress (1937-1939)

9

530

9 out of 539 total members

Federal legislation in the 1940s was dominated by World War II. Women leaders advocated on many fronts to support short- and long-term efforts at home and abroad and to secure international stability and cooperation.

Standing on Principle

Following the attack on Pearl Harbor in 1941, Rep. Jeannette Rankin, a pacifist from Montana, tried to take the House floor to oppose entering the war. Members shouted at her and told her to sit down. Despite the pressure from her House colleagues, Rankin voted her conscience. The war resolution passed the House by a vote of 388 to 1.

Source: https://history.house.gov/People/Listing/R/Rankin,-Jeannette-(R000055)/ (May 5, 2019)

Women in Military Support

In 1941 Rep. Edith Nourse Rogers of Massachusetts introduced the Women's Army Auxiliary Corps Act (P.L. 77-554), which allowed women to volunteer for non-combat roles, such as nurses, cooks, researchers, switchboard operators and clerks in the Women's Army Auxiliary Corps. Oveta Culp Hobby served as the first director of the WAAC, hiring the legal maximum of 150,000 women. They were paid less and earned fewer benefits than men, but the women who served earned the respect of those who had doubted their abilities. In 1943, the Women's Army Corps (the WACs) became part of the regular U.S. Army, not merely an auxiliary group, paving the way for other branches of the military to welcome women. Their service was critical to winning World War II.

The WACs "worked harder than men, complained less and were better disciplined."
—Gen. Douglas McArthur

Source: https://www.womensmemorial.org/history /detail/?s=wwiiwomens-army-corps (April 21, 2019)

Medical Training and Technology

Rep. Frances Bolton of Ohio authored the Nursing Training Act of 1943 (P.L. 78-74), also known as the Bolton Act, to establish the Cadet Nurse Corps to train much needed medical professionals. Unique for its time, the bill granted funds to all schools, regardless of the ethnicity of the students they served, creating opportunities for Navajo and African-American schools and propelling women into the professional middle class.[xvi] The program focused attention and funding on improving medical technology, which reaped benefits both during and long after the war.

WAC Lab Technician, 1944

Source:https://www.docsteach.org/documents/document/1-pfc-johnnie-mae-welton-negro-wac-laboratory-technician-trainee-conducts-an-experiment-in-the-serology-laboratory-sf-the-fort-jackson-station-hospital-fort-jackson-sc (National Archives, May 12, 2019)

Women in Military Service

Rep. Margaret Chase Smith of Maine gained permanent, regular and reserve status for women in all branches of the armed forces. The Women's Armed Services Integration Act of 1948 (P.L. 80-625) capped the number of women who could serve at 2% of the total forces and the number of female commissioned officers to 500, but it paved the way for women to have military careers on par with their male colleagues.

Building Global Stability

From her seat on the House Banking and Currency Committee, Connecticut Representative Chase Going Woodhouse, an economist by training, championed the country's participation in the World Bank and the International Monetary Fund (IMF). The World Bank lent funds to Western Europe for its reconstruction following World War II. Together, the two institutions promote global stability by maintaining international exchange rates, providing financial assistance to countries in need, and expanding global trade. Woodhouse reasoned, "[O]ur major economic problems are world-wide problems and ... they can be solved only by world-wide cooperation."

Source: 91 Cong. Rec. 5584 (June 5, 1945)(Statement of Rep. Woodhouse)

Women in Congress Tracker
1949 snapshot

80th Congress (1947-1949)

8

530

8 out of 538 total members

Staring Down a Bully

On June 1, 1950, freshman Senator Margaret Chase Smith of Maine summoned the courage to challenge the baseless "red scare" attacks that Joseph McCarthy had launched against scores of Americans. She warned her Senate colleagues of the danger of riding to political victory on the "Four Horsemen of Calumny - fear, ignorance, bigotry, and smear."

Those of us who shout the loudest about Americanism in making character assassinations are all too frequently those who, by our own words and acts, ignore some of the basic principles of Americanism: the right to criticize; the right to hold unpopular beliefs; the right to protest; the right of independent thought.

Source: 96 Cong. Rec. 7894 (June 1, 1950)(Statement of Sen. Margaret Chase Smith)

Veterans' Benefits

Rep. Edith Nourse Rogers of Massachusetts introduced the Veterans Readjustment Assistance Act of 1952 (P.L. 82-550) to extend the benefits of the GI Bill to veterans of the Korean War. Beginning in 1944, GI Bills have helped millions of veterans receive college degrees, training assistance, business and home loans, and unemployment insurance. A life-long champion for veterans, Rogers also proposed a cabinet-level Department of Veterans Affairs, which was eventually established in 1989.[xvii]

Federal Student Loans

Spurred by Soviet progress that led to the launch of the Sputnik satellite, the United States focused on improving science-related education. Rep. Coya Knutson of Minnesota, a former teacher, introduced what would become Title II of the National Defense Education Act of 1958 (P.L. 85-864) to provide low interest federal loans for higher education.

"Educational freedom and progress are most dear to my heart. We can't take the risk of limiting education to only those who can afford it."

–Rep. Coya Knutson

Source: 103 Cong. Rec. 2734 (February 27, 1957)
(Statement of Coya Knutson)

Women in Congress Tracker
1959 snapshot

85th Congress (1957-1959)

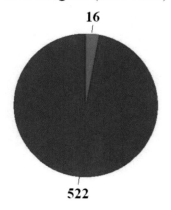

16

522

16 out of 538 total members

The 1960s were marked by federal programs that addressed poverty, healthcare, and civil rights, collectively known as the Great Society.

Equal Pay

As Executive Vice Chairman of President Kennedy's Commission on the Status of Women, labor activist Esther Peterson drafted the Equal Pay Act of 1963 (P.L. 88-38) to require women to be treated more fairly in the workplace.[xviii] Despite condemnation from business and industry, Katharine St. George of New York, Edith Green of Oregon and other congressional women lobbied for the law, which amended the Fair Labor Standards Act (see above). The Act prohibits discrimination in wages paid to employees "on the basis of sex ... for equal work on jobs the performance of which requires equal skill, effort, and responsibility, and which are performed under similar working conditions."

Gender Discrimination in Employment

Michigan Representative Martha Griffiths, a former lawyer, advocated for the inclusion of the term "sex" in a list of bases for which discrimination would be illegal under the Civil Rights Act of 1964. "The addition of that little, terrifying word 's-e-x' will not hurt this legislation in any way. In fact, it will improve it. It will make it comprehensive. It will make it logical. It will make it right."[xix] Title VII of the Civil Rights Act of 1964 (P.L. 88-352) prohibits an employer or labor union from discriminating in the hiring, compensation, promotion or training of an employee because of the employee's race, color, religion, sex, or national origin.

Food Stamps

After lobbying for a decade to create a permanent and mandatory food assistance program at the U.S. Department of Agriculture, Congresswoman Leonor Sullivan of Missouri introduced the Food Stamp Act of 1964 (P.L. 88-525). Pragmatically, she highlighted the twofold benefits of a program that would more broadly distribute the nation's food abundance - improved nutrition among low-income households and a stronger agricultural economy. To those opposed to the bill, she asked, "Who loses, then, under the plan? Hunger. Only hunger loses."[xx]

Higher Education

Edith Green of Oregon was the daughter of two teachers. She valued education, but as a student, she had to drop out of college because she could not afford it.[xxi] She spent much of her 20 years in the House striving to make higher education available to all students, regardless of income. Her Higher Education Act of 1965 (P.L. 89-329) provided federal funding for educational programs for communities and libraries. It created teaching fellowships at struggling post-secondary institutions, educational opportunity grants for needy high school graduates, and federal insurance that enabled state and non-profit student loans for higher education.

Consumer Lending

Leonor Sullivan of Missouri championed a seminal consumer protection law, the Truth in Lending Act of 1968. Part of the Consumer Credit Protection Act (P.L. 90-321), the Act requires creditors to disclose to consumers the real cost of borrowing money, including finance charges, fees, and annual percentage rates.

Speaking Out

In her first House floor speech in 1969, Shirley Chisholm, a former teacher from New York, criticized the nation's priorities, "I am, deeply, unalterably, opposed to this war in Vietnam. ... [W]e cannot squander there the lives, the money, the energy that we need desperately here, in our cities, in our schools."

Source: 115 Cong. Rec. 7765 (March 26, 1969)(Statement of Rep. Shirley Chisholm)

Shirley Chisholm Campaign Poster, 1972
Collection of the U.S. House of Representatives

Women in Congress Tracker
1969 snapshot

90th Congress (1967-1969)

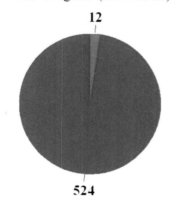

12

524

12 out of 536 total members

As their numbers slowly but steadily grew, the women of Congress gained the ability to steer legislation due to their seniority and seats on the full range of committees. They established the bipartisan Women's Caucus in 1977 to organize themselves and wield more influence.[xxii]

Credit Reports

Leonor Sullivan of Missouri introduced the Fair Credit Reporting Act to protect consumer privacy and to make consumer lending more fair. Part of a package of financial regulations in P.L. 91-508, the FCRA was the first federal law to regulate credit reports (compilations of personal information related to credit worthiness, character and reputation that are used by businesses to make decisions in employment, insurance, housing and credit). The law holds credit reporting agencies accountable for the information that they compile, and it empowers consumers to dispute the accuracy of the information.

Gender Discrimination in Education

Hawaii Representative Patsy Takemoto Mink was denied the opportunity to play full court basketball in high school because detractors believed "it was too strenuous for us."[xxiii] She introduced Title IX of the Education Amendments of 1972 (P.L. 92-318) to prohibit sex discrimination in all aspects of educational programs that receive federal funding. Title IX has had far-reaching impact, including a significant increase in funding of athletic programs for women and girls.

Susan B. Anthony Dollar Coin

Rep. Mary Rose Oakar of Ohio authored P.L. 95-447, an amendment to the Coinage Act of 1965. It ordered the Secretary of the Treasury to place the first image of a real woman on a U.S. coin. Oakar said that the coin would be a fitting tribute to Anthony's "single-minded devotion to the principle that all Americans must participate in a democracy."[xxiv]

Women in Congress Tracker
1979 snapshot

95th Congress (1977-1979)

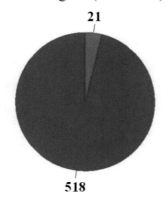

21 out of 539 total members

In 1981, Sandra Day O'Connor was appointed by President Ronald Reagan to serve as the first woman to sit on the U.S. Supreme Court.

Martin Luther King Holiday

In August 1983, Rep. Katie Hall of Indiana authored the law that established a public holiday on the third Monday in January to honor Rev. Dr. Martin Luther King, Jr. (P.L. 98-144). A national holiday honoring the late civil rights leader had been resisted for more than a decade and had even been filibustered in the Senate. Hall insisted that the Nobel Peace Prize winner deserved such commemoration because he "gave to this great Nation a new understanding of equality and justice for all."[xxv]

Small Business Support and Fiscal Responsibility

After Barbara Boxer of California famously exposed the $7,000 coffee maker purchased by the Pentagon,[xxvi] she introduced the Small Business and Federal Procurement

Competition Enhancement Act of 1984 (P.L. 98-577). The law served two purposes. It improved opportunities for small businesses to compete for major federal government contracts, and it made the federal government more fiscally accountable. The law required executive agencies to improve the transparency and availability of information in the federal contracting process.

Children's Criminal Justice

Florida Senator Paula Hawkins candidly testified that "as a victim of child sexual assault myself, I was familiar with the lack of protections afforded to children fifty years ago, and I am still saddened and astounded to learn that there is not much progress that has been made in the intervening years."[xxvii] She sponsored the Children's Criminal Justice Act (P.L. 99-401) to authorize the Secretary of Health and Human Services to give grants to States to improve the handling of child abuse cases. It funded research on causes, prevention, identification and treatment of child abuse and neglect.

Women in Congress Tracker
1989 snapshot

100th Congress (1987-1989)

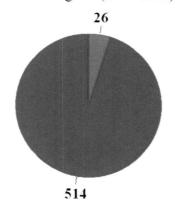

26 out of 540 total members

Record numbers of women were elected to Congress in 1992. It was known as the Year of the Woman.

Work Life Balance

Pat Schroeder of Colorado spearheaded the effort "to balance the demands of the workplace with the needs of families, to promote the stability and economic security of families, and to promote national interests in preserving family integrity."[xxviii] The Family and Medical Leave Act of 1993 (P.L. 103-3) entitles employees to 12 weeks of unpaid leave per year for the birth or adoption of a child, for the care of a child, spouse or parent, or for their own serious health condition. Reflecting on her 24 years in the House, Schroeder said, "It took nine years to get the bill signed ... . But to me, every country in the world has done this and they've done it with paid leave. We just keep pretending like, 'It's your baby or your job, lady, have a nice day.'"[xxix]

Breast Cancer Recovery

Rep. Sue Kelly of New York inserted the Women's Health and Cancer Rights Act of 1998 into the 1999 omnibus appropriations act (P.L. 105-277). It required health insurance companies to cover the costs of reconstructive surgery following a mastectomy.

Financial Crimes

Nydia Velázquez of New York observed that "the explosion of finance crimes, money laundering, credit card fraud and counterfeiting is draining our communities of valuable resources."[xxx] She authored the Money Laundering and Financial Crimes Strategy Act of 1998 (P.L. 105-310) so that "Federal, State, and local law enforcement agencies will at last be able to coordinate their efforts to combat this rising criminal tide."[xxxi] The law directed the President to work with the Secretary of the Treasury and the Attorney General to develop a national strategy to combat money laundering. It authorized grants for state and local law enforcement agencies to support "financial crime-free communities."

Women in Congress Tracker
1999 snapshot

105th Congress (1997-1999)

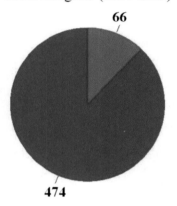

66

474

66 out of 540 total members

AMBER Alerts

Sens. Dianne Feinstein of California and Kay Bailey Hutchison of Texas created a national system to help locate abducted children whose kidnappers may have crossed state lines. Named for a nine-year old Texas girl who was abducted and murdered in 1996, the law (Title III of P.L. 108-21) provided funds to help states, cities and communities distribute alerts when a child has been abducted. Today, AMBER Alerts are broadcast through radio, television, road signs, cellular phones, and other devices in all 50 states, the District of Columbia, Indian country, Puerto Rico, the U.S. Virgin Islands, and 27 other countries. According to the National Center for Missing and Exploited Children, AMBER Alerts have resulted in the safe return of more than 957 children.[xxxii]

Genetic Discrimination

As genetic information became more widely available, Rep. Louise Slaughter of New York and Sen. Olympia Snowe of Maine feared a new form of discrimination in employment and health insurance. Snowe reasoned, "[I]n the past Congress has had to act to address existing discrimination. But today we are acting proactively to address genetic bias, before discrimination becomes entrenched."[xxxiii] Their ideas became the Genetic Information Nondiscrimination Act of 2008 (P.L. 110–233).

Breast Cancer Research

Suspecting that environmental factors such as cigarette smoking, excessive alcohol consumption, poor diet, lack of exercise, excessive sunlight exposure, and certain drugs, viruses, and chemicals may be contributing causes of cancer, New York Representative Nita Lowey sponsored the Breast Cancer and Environmental Research Act of 2008 (P.L. 110–354). The law authorized $40,000,000 to establish a coordinating committee of doctors and researchers to develop a comprehensive strategy to advance research and disseminate information on environmental and genomic causes of breast cancer.

Fair Pay

The Lilly Ledbetter Fair Pay Act of 2009 (P.L. 111–2) was Maryland Senator Barbara Mikulski's response to the Supreme Court's 2007 decision in *Ledbetter v. Goodyear Tire & Rubber Co.*, 550 U.S. 618 (2007). The Court found that Lilly Ledbetter had earned less money over 19 years as a Goodyear supervisor because she was a woman. However, the Court ruled that she had no relief under Title VII of the Civil Rights Act of 1964 (see above) because Title VII claims had to be brought within 180 days of her employer's decision to pay her unlawfully; Ledbetter had filed her claim too late.[xxxiv]

Justice Ruth Bader Ginsburg dissented, asserting that each smaller paycheck that Ledbetter received was a new act of unlawful discrimination and that Ledbetter had a remedy under Title VII. Ginsburg concluded that "the ball is in Congress' court" to correct the Court's "cramped interpretation of Title VII." Sen. Mikulski took the ball and ran with it. The Ledbetter Act made clear that each discriminatory paycheck is a separate and actionable unlawful event.

9/11 Recovery

Rep. Carolyn Maloney and Sen. Kirsten Gillibrand of New York spearheaded the effort to pass the James Zadroga 9/11 Health and Compensation Act of 2010 (P.L. 111–347). The law established a federal health and compensation program for emergency responders and community members who suffered illness or injury due to the terrorist attacks of September 11, 2001.

Women in Congress Tracker
2009 snapshot

110th Congress (2007-2009)

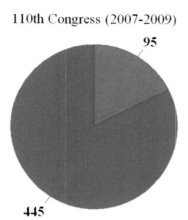

95 out of 540 members total

As the number of women serving in Congress increases, so does the breadth of issues that they tackle.

A Tribute to Four Young Girls

Rep. Terri Sewell of Alabama introduced the law to award posthumously a Congressional Gold Medal to Addie Mae Collins, Denise McNair, Carole Robertson, and Cynthia Wesley (P.L. 113-11). It commemorated the 50th anniversary of the murder of the girls as they prepared for Sunday school at Sixteenth Street Baptist Church in Birmingham, Alabama. The bombing of the church was an act of terrorism that shook the world and galvanized efforts to pass the Civil Rights Act of 1964 and the Voting Rights Act of 1965.

In 2013 New Hampshire became the first state to have an all-female Congressional delegation -- Sens. Jeanne Shaheen and Kelly Ayotte and Reps. Ann McLane Kuster and Carol Shea-Porter.

Disabled Veterans' Assistance

Rep. Tulsi Gabbard, a former member of the Hawaii National Guard, authored the Helping Heroes Fly Act (P.L. 113-27) to assist wounded military veterans in the airport security screening process. The law directed the Assistant Secretary of Homeland Security to develop and implement a process to facilitate expedited and private passenger screening for severely injured or disabled veterans or members of the armed services, when possible.

Natural Disaster Recovery

Ranking Member of the House Small Business Committee Nydia Velázquez of New York authored the Recovery Improvement for Small Entities (RISE) After Disaster Act of 2015 (P.L. 114-88). The law improved the Small Business Administration's response to Superstorm Sandy. It extended the ability of small business owners, homeowners, and renters impacted by the storm to apply for low interest loans from the SBA to get back on their feet. To address inadequate performance by the SBA, the law required improvements in the timeliness and transparency of SBA loan processing and disaster planning.

Breastfeeding Support

When safety restrictions made air travel increasingly difficult for families with infants, Rep. Jaime Herrera Beutler of Washington and Sen. Kelly Ayotte of New Hampshire sought common sense solutions. The Bottles and Breastfeeding Equipment Screening Act (P.L. 114-293) required the Transportation Security Administration and private security companies to train airport screeners on the appropriate handling of infant formula and breastfeeding equipment under the 3-1-1 Liquids Rule Exemption.

Ocean Conservation

American Samoa Representative Amata Coleman Radewagen introduced the Ensuring Access to Pacific Fisheries Act (P.L. 114-327) to improve the management of international waters. It authorizes the U.S. to participate in and enforce the regulations of the Conventions on the Conservation and Management of High Seas Fisheries Resources in the North Pacific Ocean and in the South Pacific Ocean. Nations that are parties to the Conventions are committed to the twin goals of ensuring the long-term conservation and sustainable use of fisheries resources and safeguarding marine ecosystems.

Law Enforcement Support

Reps. Val Demings of Florida and Susan Brooks of Indiana sponsored the Law Enforcement Mental Health and Wellness Act of 2017 (P.L. 115-113) to provide for the mental health needs of police officers. It directed the Attorney General and the Secretary of Health and Human Services to study and implement techniques, therapies and wellness checks to help federal, state, local and tribal law enforcement officers deal with mental trauma. Former Orlando Police Chief Demings hailed the new law and vowed, "We cannot ask our officers to do this work while failing to cope with the consequences. We must take care of them so they can take care of us."[xxxv]

In 2016 Sen. Hillary Rodham Clinton became the first woman to be a major party's nominee for president. Clinton won a majority of the popular vote -- 65.8 million to Donald Trump's 62.9 million -- but she lost the election because she did not win a majority of the electoral votes.

Source: https://transition.fec.gov/pubrec/fe2016/2016presgeresults.pdf

Women in Congress Tracker
2019 snapshot

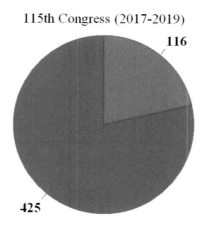

115th Congress (2017-2019)

116

425

116 out of 541 total members

PART III
THE NEXT 100 YEARS

Since gaining the right to vote in 1920, American women have organized, won public office and written landmark laws. Their ideas were often disparaged and dismissed, but their persistence ultimately made government more responsive to the needs of the nation and the world. Women have been the driving force behind laws that strengthened our social safety net, protected our children, and honored our heroes. They legislated for fairness and equal opportunity, for investments in America's collective future, and for global stability. Their once-maligned ideas are now woven into the fabric of American life. Much has been gained by having women at the table.

As we celebrate 100 years of suffrage, there are 131 senators, representatives and delegates serving in Congress, comprising the largest delegation of women yet. But in a nation that is 50.8% women,[xxxvi] they amount to just 24% of the body that makes the nation's laws.

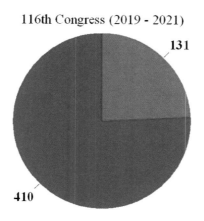

116th Congress (2019 - 2021)

131

410

131 out of 541 total members

Social scientists know that numbers matter. In the corporate arena, many studies have shown that having more women on corporate boards improves working environments, financial performance, and social responsibility; it leads to more innovation and better deliberations.[xxxvii] If the dynamics of the corporate board room hold true in the halls of government, American women remain a valuable and untapped resource.

Let us carry forward the wisdom of the suffragists, who knew that government only represents those who have a voice. Let us embrace the civic duties to be informed, to participate, and, above all, to exercise the precious right to vote. When we do, all of "We the People" will be able to work together to form a more perfect union.

For the next 100 years, make every vote count.

What about the ERA?

Since the 1920s, versions of an Equal Rights Amendment to the Constitution have floundered. It might simply affirm, "Women shall have equal rights in the United States and every place subject to its jurisdiction. Equality of rights under the law shall not be denied or abridged by the United States or by any State on account of sex." Do we need it?

Endnotes

[i] "Abigail Adams to John Adams, 31 March 1776," *Founders Online*, National Archives, version of January 18, 2019, https://founders.archives.gov/documents/Adams/04-01-02-0241

[ii] "John Adams to Abigail Adams, 14 April 1776," *Founders Online*, National Archives, version of January 18, 2019, https://founders.archives.gov/documents/Adams/04-01-02-0248

[iii] "John Adams to James Sullivan, 26 May 1776," *Founders Online*, National Archives, version of January 18, 2019, https://founders.archives.gov/documents/Adams/06-04-02-0091

[iv] Article I, section 2, U.S. Constitution

[v] Amendment XIV, section 2, U.S. Constitution (Federal representation would be reduced for any state that denied the vote to any male citizen 21 years or older.)

[vi] Petition to Congress, December 1871, https://www.archives.gov/education/lessons/woman-suffrage/petition-to-congress (April 16, 2019)

[vii] *An Account of the Proceedings of the Trial of Susan B. Anthony*, National American Woman Suffrage Association Collection, Library of Congress, https://www.loc.gov/resource/rbnawsa.n2152 (April 16, 2019)

[viii] https://www.archives.gov/files/publications/prologue/2003/fall/19th-amendment-gives-women-the-vote.pdf (April 16, 2019)

[ix] *Id.*

[x] https://history.house.gov/People/Listing/R/Robertson,-Alice-Mary-(R000318)/ (April 16, 2019)

[xi] *American Citizenship Rights of Women, Hearing Before a Subcommittee of the Senate Committee on Immigration*, 72nd Cong., 2nd session, March 2, 1933, 27-29

[xii] *Id.* at 28

[xiii] "The Young Crusader, Women's Christian Temperance Magazine for Children, 1934," *Document Bank of Virginia*, http://edu.lva.virginia.gov/dbva/items/show/230 (May 5, 2019)

[xiv] https://history.house.gov/Exhibitions-and-Publications/WIC/Historical-Essays/No-Lady/Legislative-Interests/ (April 16, 2019)

[xv] "Social Security Pioneers, Frances Perkins," https://www.ssa.gov/history/fperkins.html (May 5, 2019)

[xvi] Alexandra Lord, "Creating the Cadet Nurse Corps for World War II, http://americanhistory.si.edu/blog/creating-cadet-nurse-corps-world-war-ii (April 22, 2019)

[xvii] *Women in Congress 1917-2006,* https://www.govinfo.gov/content/pkg/GPO-CDOC-108hdoc223/pdf/GPO-CDOC-108hdoc223.pdf, 74 (April 24, 2019)

[xviii] https://www.nps.gov/articles/equal-pay-act.htm (April 25, 2019)

[xix] 110 Cong. Rec. 2580 (February 8, 1964)(Statement of Rep. Martha Griffiths)

[xx] 110 Cong. Rec. 7133 (April 7, 1964)(Statement of Rep. Leonor Sullivan)

[xxi] Mina Naderpoor, "The Mother of Higher Education," http://www.uoalumni.com/s/1540/uoaa/index.aspx?sid=1540&gid=3&pgid=6450 (May 10, 2019)

[xxii] *Women in Congress,* 2

[xxiii] Memorial Addresses and Other Tributes Hon. Patsy T. Mink, Cong. Rec. (September 30, 2002)(Statement of Rep. Eddie Bernice Johnson), 26

[xxiv] 124 Cong. Rec. 17712 (June 14, 1978)(Statement of Rep. Mary Rose Oakar)

[xxv] 129 Cong. Rec. 22208 (August 2, 1983)(Statement of Rep. Katie Hall)

[xxvi] *Major Fraud Act of 1988, Hearings Before Subcommittee on Crime, House Judiciary Committee,* 100th Cong., 1st session, December 3, 1987, 124

[xxvii] *Federal Assistance to States to Prevent the Abuse of Children in Child Care Facilities, Hearing Before the Subcommittee on Juvenile Justice, Senate Judiciary Committee,* 98th Cong., 2nd session, September 18, 1984, 54-5

[xxviii] 29 U.S.C. §2601(b)(1)

[xxix] Oral History Interview, Final Edited Transcript, June 3, 2015, https://history.house.gov/Oral-History/Women/Representative-Schroeder/, 35 (April 27, 2019)

[xxx] 143 Cong. Rec. H3280 (June 4, 1997)(Statement of Rep. Nydia Velázquez)

[xxxi] *Id.*

[xxxii] https://www.missingkids.org/gethelpnow/amber (May 1, 2019)

[xxxiii] 153 Cong. Rec. S846 (January 22, 2007)(Statement of Sen. Olympia Snowe)

xxxiv Both the majority opinion and the dissent by Justice Ginsburg
noted that Ledbetter may have had an easier burden under the Equal Pay
Act (see above), but a claim under that law was not before the Court.

xxxv https://demings.house.gov/media/press-releases/rep-demings-
law-enforcement-mental-health-bill-signed-law (May 16, 2019)

xxxvi Women's History Month: 2019,
https://www.census.gov/newsroom/facts-for-features/2019/womens-
history.html (May 5, 2019)

xxxvii Antonia L. García-Izquierdo, Carlos Fernández-Méndez, and
Rubén Arrondo-Garcia, "Gender Diversity on Boards of Directors and
Remuneration Committees," *Frontiers in Psychology*, 2018; 9: 1351
(https://www.ncbi.nlm.nih.gov/pmc/articles/PMC6108384/)(May 5,
2019)

Made in the USA
Middletown, DE
17 July 2019